The Outdoor
Adventure
Handbook

The Outdoor Adventure Handbook

Hugh McManners

A DK PUBLISHING BOOK

Editor Patricia Grogan **Art Editor** Lesley Betts

Project Editor Fiona Robertson

US Editor Camela Decaire

Photography Andy Crawford

Production Charlotte Traill

Deputy Editorial Director Sophie Mitchell
Deputy Art Director Miranda Kennedy

The outdoor adventurers:
Nadia Barak, Jessie Clark, Ryan Davies,
Johnathan Green, Sayed Meah, Lauren Shaw

First American Edition
2 4 6 8 10 9 7 5 3 1

Published in the United States by DK Publishing, Inc.
95 Madison Avenue, New York, NY 10016

Copyright © 1996 Dorling Kindersley Limited, London
Text copyright © 1996 Hugh McManners

Published in Great Britain by Dorling Kindersley Ltd.
Distributed by Houghton Mifflin Company, Boston.

A CIP catalog record is available from the Library of Congress.
ISBN 0-7894-0468-0 (paperback)
ISBN 0-7894-1035-4 (hardcover)

Color reproduction by Colourscan, Singapore
Printed in Hong Kong by Wing King Tong

The author would like to dedicate this book to his two sons,
William and Joseph, with all his love.

Contents

6
How to use this book

8
Outdoor clothes

10
Your outdoor gear

12
Packing your outdoor gear

14
Choosing your campsite

16
Building a shelter

18
Living in your camp

20
Clean and tidy

22
Sleeping outdoors

24
Making a fire

26
Cooking on a fire

28
All-in-one stew

30
More recipe ideas

32
Making camp equipment

34
Water in your camp

36
Using a compass

38
Reading a map

40
Finding your way

42
Using the Sun and stars

44
Messages and trails

46
Plant watch

48
Animal watch

50
Weather watch

52
Using a penknife safely

54
Useful knots I

56
Useful knots II

58
First aid I

60
First aid II

62
Outdoor Code &
Useful addresses

64
Index & Acknowledgments

How to use this book

This book contains all the information you need to enjoy the outdoors. It will help you understand and avoid the problems that could arise, and ensure that your trips are always safe and successful. Enjoy your adventures!

Getting out

Planning is the key to a successful trip. Think carefully about what you are going to do and what you will need. The more trips you go on, the more experienced you will become, but for now, use this book to get the best possible start!

Look on page 8 to find out how to roll your clothes, preparing them to pack in your backpack.

Page 13 will show you how to carry your backpack safely.

Setting up camp

Find out what to avoid at your campsite on page 14.

Learn how to organize everything inside your tent on page 18.

When choosing a campsite, you need to know how to look for a safe, comfortable site, and know how to recognize the kinds of places to avoid. Trying to move a poorly placed camp at night is very inconvenient, and can even be dangerous.

Cooking outdoors

For delicious meals and enjoyable evenings, it is hard to beat a campfire. However, fires can spread easily, so it is important that you learn how to build and light them safely. When handling hot liquids and food, you should be sure that you use the right equipment to avoid burning yourself.

Build a tepee fire following the instructions on page 24.

Try some of the alternative cooking methods shown on page 27.

Living outdoors

Look on page 33 to learn how to make a stool for your camp.

Page 34 shows you how to ensure that you always have clean water in your camp.

If you are going to live outdoors for a while, you can make equipment for your camp. It is also important to camp near a supply of water because you will not be able to take all the water you need with you.

Navigation outdoors

Being able to navigate, or find your way, accurately is an important outdoor skill. It keeps you from getting lost and also enables you to reach your destination by other routes. Once you have learned how to read a map correctly, you can even try making your own!

Make your own compass by following the instructions on page 37.

Learn what a roun card is used for ar how to make one on page 40.

Observing nature

Nature can provide you with many clues about your environment. For example, plants can show you which direction you are heading and insects can indicate where the nearest water is. The clouds in the sky can help you predict the weather.

Learn the difference between a hopping print and a wading print on page 48.

See how to predict the weather using the clouds on page 50.

Important techniques

Using a knife, tying knots, and basic first aid are skills that you have to learn how to do properly. This book contains detailed sections showing exactly what you need to know – particularly how to take care of someone who is injured.

Learn how to sharpen a penknife on page 53.

Find out when and how to put someone in the recovery position on page 61.

Find groups in your area that organize outdoor activities on page 63.

The index on page 64 shows you where to find everything in this book.

Reference pages

The outdoors is a wonderful place. It must be taken care of not only so that we can enjoy it, but also so that others may have as much fun as we do. The Outdoor Code tells you exactly how to do this.

How to use each page

Each double-page in this book tells you everything you need to know about one subject. The introduction gives you an overview, and the step-by-step instructions show you how to make and do everything.

Star symbol
This symbol appears next to important safety points.

Knot symbol
You will see this symbol when you need to tie a knot.

Penknife symbol
Every time you need to use a penknife, you will see this symbol.

Locater picture
This picture sums up what is being shown on the page.

Materials box
Look here to see the materials you will need.

Ecology points
These symbols are found next to points about our environment.

Hints and tips
Each hints and tips box is packed with useful informaton.

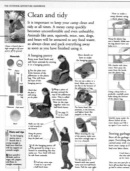

Boot-print symbol
This symbol appears next to a useful tip.

Step-by-step instructions show you how to make useful items for your outdoor adventures.

Hints and tips boxes have a picture of a boy or girl.

Boxed instructions
These instructions give you details on how to make and do the activities.

Extra information
The bottom right-hand pages often have additional or new information about the subject.

Outdoor clothes

The secret to staying warm in the cold and cool in the heat is wearing lots of thin layers of loose-fitting clothing. Air is trapped between each layer of clothing and is warmed up by your body heat. You can add or remove layers if you start to feel cold or hot. Trapping your body heat in this way is called insulation.

Water- and windproof jackets keep you dry and protected from the weather.

Packing for winter weather

Pack several layers of underwear, T-shirts, and shirts. Lots of thin, loose clothing is better than a little thick, bulky gear, which is difficult to dry out.

How to roll your clothes for packing in your backpack

Take plenty of T-shirts.

Pack two or three long-sleeved shirts.

Warm, loose-fitting pants are vital.

Lay your clothes out flat in an oblong shape. If you are folding a top, fold the sleeves inward.

Thermal underwear is good for sleeping in.

A warm sweater is ideal for wearing on cool evenings.

Pack several pairs of underpants.

Starting at the bottom, roll up each item of clothing. Do not roll the clothes too tightly.

Take several pairs of thick wool or cotton socks.

Wear hiking boots or sturdy shoes.

A spare pair of lighter shoes is very useful.

Your rolled clothes will take up less room in your backpack, and should not get too creased.

Hints and tips

Avoid wearing thermal underwear when you are walking because it may make you too hot.

When you are resting, put on extra layers and a warm hat before you start feeling cold.

Wet weather clothes

You need clothes that will keep you dry, but do not trap heat and moisture.

Lace secures gaiter to your leg.

Gaiters stop water from running into your boots and making your feet wet.

Wear waterproof pants whenever you may be working on the ground.

Wear gaiters when walking in wet weather. They are much cooler than waterproof pants.

Winter clothes

Wear lots of thin layers. The outer ones should have zippers so that you can open them if you get too hot.

A warm hat is vital – up to half your body heat is lost through your head and shoulders.

Gloves and a scarf will keep you warm.

Watch out for water running off your jacket and onto your pants and socks.

Wear two pairs of socks when it is very cold.

Summer clothes

Shorts and T-shirts are great for warm weather, but in hot sunshine wear light, long-sleeved tops and pants.

A cap with a visor keeps the sun off your face.

Wear plenty of sunscreen in sunny weather.

Loose-fitting cotton T-shirt

Wear light colors in very hot weather to reflect the heat.

Thick socks will make your boots more comfortable.

How to protect your neck from the sun using a dish towel

Place the dish towel over your head, making sure it covers the sides and back of your neck.

Put a cap with a visor on over the dish towel. The visor will protect your face.

Secure the dish towel by carefully safety-pinning it around the bottom of the cap.

If it is very hot, soak the dish towel in cold water first.

Packing for summer weather

Cotton clothes are ideal. You need fewer layers in the summer than in the winter, but do not forget to pack warm clothes, too, in case it gets cold at night.

Take a few cotton undershirts.

Pack long- and short-sleeved tops.

Take a warm sweater for the evenings.

Pack several pairs of cotton underpants.

Spare shoes; sneakers are ideal.

Shorts are perfect for warm days.

Thick, cotton socks will insulate your feet from hot ground.

Lightweight pants will dry out easily if they get wet.

Wear hiking boots or sturdy shoes.

Your outdoor gear

It is easy to pack too much, and it is very hard to carry it all. Think carefully about what you are going to do, then take only the bare minimum. Your survival gear is the most important, so always allow room for it in your backpack. Try to find several different uses for everything else that you take with you.

If in doubt, you probably do not need it, so leave it out.

Your survival gear

This is the most important gear to take with you. Keep it in waterproof containers and make sure you know where all of it is at all times.

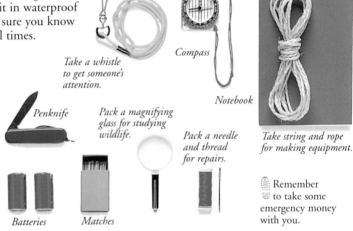

Take a whistle to get someone's attention.

Compass

Flashlight

Notebook

Pen

Penknife

Pack a magnifying glass for studying wildlife.

Pack a needle and thread for repairs.

Take string and rope for making equipment.

Remember to take some emergency money with you.

Candle

Batteries

Matches

Your shelter gear

This gear will keep you warm and dry, so it is important to maintain it carefully.

A first aid kit is vital on all trips.

Use garbage bags to make your backpack waterproof.

Sleeping bag

Keep the tent poles together.

Check the tent has no holes in it before setting off.

A sleeping mat will keep you warm at night.

A sheet to make a sheet bag

Take a ground sheet if your tent does not have one.

Your cooking gear

You can get away with just taking a wooden spoon, mug, plate, cooking pot with a lid, and a can opener. If you have room, take foil with you to wrap and cook food in.

Take a set of cooking pots with lids and handles.

Foil is always handy.

Pack a pot holder if your set does not have a handle.

A wooden spatula is useful for lifting fish off a grill.

A water bottle is always useful.

Fork

Spoon

Knife

Wooden spoon

Can opener

Use a bowl for soup and cereal.

Plastic plates do not heat up as quickly as metal plates.

Take a plastic mug for hot drinks.

Bowl

Plate

Clean-up gear

Clean up after every meal. It is important to wash everything so you do not attract animals.

Dishwashing liquid

Scouring pad

Dish towel to dry up with

...owl to wash up in

Your washing gear

Do not forget to pack your toiletries. Keep them all together in a clean waterproof bag.

Packing items like your shampoo in small containers will save space in your backpack.

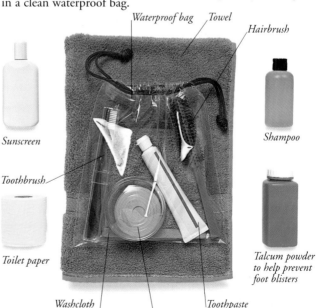

Waterproof bag   *Towel*

Hairbrush

Sunscreen

Shampoo

Toothbrush

Toilet paper

Talcum powder to help prevent foot blisters

Washcloth

Soap

Toothpaste

Packing your outdoor gea

Make sure everything in your backpack is waterproof by packing it in plastic bags. Group things that you use together in the same bag so that you can find them easily. Pack all of these bags inside your lined backpack; if they are attached to the outside, they could fall off or get damaged.

Line your backpack with two large garbage bags to make it waterproof.

How to pack

The main rules to remember are to put the heaviest things at the top of your backpack, the lightest, bulkiest things at the bottom, and the things that you need to get at quickly in the side pockets. Pack your sleeping bag in the bottom of your backpack first. Do not forget to wrap it in a waterproof bag. Then add other light items, such as tent poles.

Weekend packs
Use a small pack for short trips since you will not need to take so much with you.

Backpacks
Choose a backpack that is not too large, otherwise you may be tempted to pack too much and will not be able to carry it all.

Cooking equipment, such as a pot, is a heavy item.

Toilet paper

Keep the first aid kit handy at all times.

Keep your toiletries together in a waterproof bag.

Sun block

Plates

Water bottle

Pack your survival gear in a side pocket so you can get to it easily.

Penknife

Whistle

Keep your backpack full so the heavy items stay at the top.

Pack the tent poles higher than your clothes, which are lighter.

Tent poles and pegs should be packed in the same bag.

Pack things inside each other to save space.

Use soft items to pad out the back of your backpack.

Pack string and rope for making equipment.

Pack spare shoes with the soles facing outward.

Roll your clothes and f them in plastic bags.

⭐ Make sure there are no sha edges digging i your back.

The bottom of the backpack is filled out with the sleeping bag.

How to make a bag to carry lighter items

Wrap some string around a pebble placed in the corner of a strong bag and tie two half-hitch knots.

Join the string to 3 ft (1 m) of thick rope with a sheet bend knot to make the shoulder strap.

Pack everything evenly into the bag. Gather the top of the bag and place a pebble on top.

Fold over the top of the bag, wrap some string around the pebble, and tie two half-hitch knots.

Tie this string to the rope with a sheet bend knot. Sling the bag diagonally across your back.

See page 55 to learn the half-hitch knot and a sheet bend.

Making a bag

You never know when you may need an extra bag. Follow the instructions on the left to make a bag that you can use on short day trips, or for collecting firewood.

Make sure everything is spread out evenly through the bag.

Avoid sharp items that may make a hole in the bag.

You can buy special backpack liners, which are ideal for making bags.

👣 Pad the shoulder strap of the bag with leaves.

Carrying your backpack

Backpacks are often heavy. Because of this, it is important to carry them correctly so that you do not hurt yourself. Adjust your pack so that it is as high up as possible to stop the weight from pulling on your shoulders.

Adjustable straps allow the backpack to be carried high on the back.

Tighten and loosen the shoulder straps whenever you feel uncomfortable.

Waist belts help keep the weight off your shoulders.

👣 When walking downhill or crossing rivers, undo the waist belt in case you stumble and have to drop the backpack.

How to make matches waterproof with wax candles

Using a lighted candle, drip wax over the heads of a box of matches, laid side by side.

When the wax has cooled, separate each match. Before using them, scrape the wax off the head of each match.

⭐ You may need to ask an adult to help you.

How to adjust a backpack to make it comfortable

To open the waist belt, squeeze in the side of the buckle with the "teeth." This will release the clasp.

To tighten the waist belt, hold the buckle and pull the strap to the side until the belt is secure.

Tighten the shoulder straps by lifting the edge of the buckle up and pulling the strap down.

Choosing your campsite

It is very important to choose a safe and comfortable place for your campsite, even if you are only going to spend one night outdoors. Look for a dry area that is slightly raised, so that if it rains, the ground will not get boggy. Also try to avoid stony ground because it is very uncomfortable to sleep on.

Always take the time to find a good spot for your campsite.

If you are camping on anyone's property, always get permission from the land owner.

Avoid camping in a basin where flood water could flow.

Your campsite should be close to a supply of fresh, clean water.

Bushes and low trees will give you shelter from wind and rain.

Keep food well away from animals and your tent.

Pack away your clothes as soon as they are dry

Keep food cool by placing it under the shade of a tree.

Choose a windy spot to tie a clothesline.

If you have a camp toilet, make sure it is downwind from your tent.

Avoid camping in fields with animals.

Flatten the spot you will put up your tent on by removing stones and twigs, and stamping down any bumps.

If you are camping near mountains, do not put up your tent in the path of a possible avalanche.

If you are camping near the ocean, avoid low-lying ground where the tide might reach you.

Do not put up your tent under trees with branches that could snap off in a strong wind.

Sleeping on a slope is not easy or comfortable, so try to put up your tent on fairly level ground.

Ridge tents, like the one pictured below, are ideal for most conditions.

Choosing a tent for the right conditions

A domed tent is light and spacious. If it is tied down securely, it is ideal for mountainous areas.

A tunnel tent can be used on grass or in rocky river valleys. It can withstand strong winds.

Ridge tent

Always position your campfire downwind from your tent.

Make sure sparks from your fire cannot reach your tent.

Choose level ground for your cooking area and tent.

Put up your tent so that the entrance faces away from the wind.

15

Building a shelter

When you are camping outdoors, you may need a shelter for protection from heavy rain, strong winds, or hot sunshine. If you do not have a tent, you can make this shelter using everyday materials. Put it up on flat ground, in a sheltered place that is protected from the wind.

Sharing a two-person shelter is not just fun, it will also keep you warm.

Materials

Tennis ball cut in half   *Penknife*

Matches

Sticks   *Ground sheet*

Sheet of plastic

Rope

Pebbles

Stones or bricks

Hints and tips

Always use a flashlight to light your shelter. Matches and candles can be dangerous – their flames could set fire to your shelter.

In high winds, go outside often to check the ropes around the edge of your shelter are tight.

Making your shelter

This two-person shelter can stand on hard or soft ground. It should be wide enough for three people to lie close together in it.

1 Get a strong sheet of plastic 6.5 ft x 13 ft (2 m x 4 m). Open it out and lay it on the ground.

See page 54 to tie a reef knot.

2 Attach a length of rope to each corner and the centers of the longer sides. Use round pebbles to secure the ropes, as shown right.

Tie a reef knot in the ropes.

You could also attach the ropes to tent pegs.

Leave some rope between the stone and sheet.

3 Wrap the ropes loosely around large stones or bricks to hold the sheet down. Tie half-hitch knots in the wrapped ropes to secure them to the stones or bricks.

How to prepare ropes and attach them to your shelter

If you are using rope made of artificial fibers, carefully trim the ends with a penknife.

Melt the ends of the rope with a match. This will seal the fibers together and stop them from fraying.

Wrap the sheet around two or three pebbles in the middle of each long side and at each corner.

Wrap a piece of rope around the sheet and set of pebbles. Sec: ropes with a reef

How to anchor your shelter and protect the top of it

Wrap the loose end of each rope around a heavy stone or brick and secure it with a half-hitch knot.

Using a penknife, slice a tennis ball in half and put each half onto the end of a stick.

If one stone is not heavy enough, put another stone on top of it.

See page 52 to learn how to use a penknife safely.

4 With the cut tennis balls on the two sticks (see the detailed instructions, left), insert the tops of the sticks, one at each end of the sheet. Push the sticks into the ground and pull the stones out to make the sheet form a triangular shape.

See page 55 to tie a half-hitch knot.

The tennis ball will prevent the stick from making a hole in the sheet.

The sticks should stand upright.

Adjust the stones to pull the ropes tight around the sheet.

The ridge of the tent must be pulled straight.

Wrap the rope around the stone until it is the correct length.

5 Adjust the stones so that the sides of the shelter are pulled tight and straight. This will ensure that rainwater does not collect on the shelter. Make your shelter more comfortable by putting a waterproof ground sheet inside it. Use a piece of plastic or canvas on wet ground. You could use a rug on dry ground.

Make a shallow trench around the tent to guide rainwater away.

Arrange the ground sheet so that it does not stick out; otherwise it may collect rainwater.

Which tent?

There are many kinds of tents, each suitable for different conditions. Some are better for snowy conditions, and others have more room. A basic ridge tent, like this one, can be used anywhere from a mountainside to your backyard.

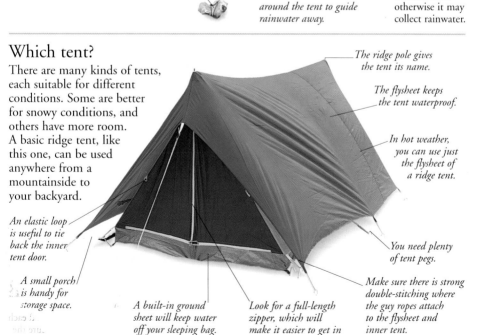

The ridge pole gives the tent its name.

The flysheet keeps the tent waterproof.

In hot weather, you can use just the flysheet of a ridge tent.

An elastic loop is useful to tie back the inner tent door.

A small porch is handy for storage space.

A built-in ground sheet will keep water off your sleeping bag.

Look for a full-length zipper, which will make it easier to get in and out of the tent.

You need plenty of tent pegs.

Make sure there is strong double-stitching where the guy ropes attach to the flysheet and inner tent.

Living in your camp

The secret to being comfortable outdoors is to be well organized. Have a place for everything so that nothing gets lost or wet. Whether you are spending just one day or several days outdoors, keep everything that you are not actually using packed, and have set places for everything else.

Hang your boots on sticks pushed into the ground inside your tent porch.

Materials

Twigs

Stick

Rubber bands

Penknife

Strong rope for clothes-line

Rope for hand rail

Organizing items in your tent

There is not much room in your tent, so it is important to organize everything carefully. Place things you will need at night close to the head of your sleeping bag. Keep everything else away from the walls of your tent.

Keep your backpack either in the porch of your tent or just outside.

Have your water bottle handy in case you get thirsty.

Keep any snacks in a sealed bag outside your tent.

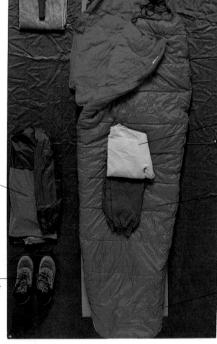

Put your flashlight beside your sleeping bag so that you can find it in the dark.

Pack away your cooking equipment at night in the porch of your tent.

Lay out your sleeping bag with the head facing the door of your tent.

Anything that touches the walls of your tent will get wet, so place your waterproof clothes here.

Place your sleeping clothes inside your sleeping bag.

Store your valuables inside your sleeping bag or under your pillow at night.

Keep your spare shoes at the foot of your tent.

Put your sleeping bag on a foam sleeping mat.

Hints and tips

Hanging a flashlight from the pole at the front of your tent will enable you to light up your tent at night.

When sharing your tent, place the sleeping bags side by side with your clothes in the middle.

Making a clothesline

It is important to keep everything clean and fresh when you are outdoors, and this includes your clothes. You can use a clothesline not only to dry washed clothes, but also to air everything, including your sleeping bag!

See page 54 to tie a reef knot.

1 Tie one end of some strong rope around your tent pole. Secure the rope with a reef knot.

Use rope that will not stretch when you put clothes on it.

Position the front of your tent near a tree with strong branches.

Choose a tree far enough away to provide sufficient hanging space for your clothes.

Use your clothesline to air your equipment regularly.

2 Tie the other end of the rope to a strong branch. Wrap the rope around the branch twice and secure it with a reef knot.

Choose a branch that is about shoulder height.

Your hand rail should be at waist height.

Pull the rope tight.

Hang your clothes out to dry and air on breezy days.

3 With another piece of rope, make a hand rail that you can use as a guide to your camp toilet at night. Attach the rope in exactly the same way you did for the clothesline.

Make your clothes secure on the clothesline using clothespins.

Making a clothespin

If you do not take clothespins with you, or you do not have enough, you can always make some when you are outdoors.

See page 52 to learn how to use a penknife safely.

1 Find two twigs about 2½ in (10 cm) long. Using a penknife, carefully flatten one long edge of each stick.

2 With the flattened edges facing each other, wrap a rubber band tightly around the two sticks.

3 The rubber band will allow you to pull the sticks slightly apart to fit over the clothesline and then spring back again.

Choose a branch that is high enough to lift your pantry off the ground.

Clean and tidy

It is important to keep your camp clean and tidy at all times. A messy camp quickly becomes uncomfortable and even unhealthy. Animals like ants, squirrels, mice, rats, dogs, and bears will be attracted to any food waste, so always clean and pack everything away as soon as you have finished using it.

Materials

Plate

Rope

Plastic bags

Fork

Garbage bag

Pillowcase   Dish towel

Bowl

Hints and tips

Tie the hanging pantry onto a branch that is strong enough to hold your food but will not support an animal's weight.

Store powdery foods, such as sugar, salt, pepper, and flour, in airtight containers.

A hanging pantry

Keep your food fresh and safe from animals by storing it in a hanging pantry.

1 Put the plate into the bottom of the pillowcase or the plastic bag. This will form the base of the hanging pantry.

Check that the food is still sitting on the plate.

2 Wrap a piece of rope around the top of the pillowcase twice. This is called two round turns. Now tie the rope together with two half-hitch knots.

See page 55 to tie a half-hitch knot.

Make sure the rope is tied securely to the branch.

Hang the pantry in the shade to keep the food cool.

3 Lift the hanging pantry off the ground by tying it to a branch or something else that sticks out. Your food will now be safe from animals.

Coil any extra rope and tie it up with a half-hitch knot.

More details on how to make the hanging pantry

You can use a plate or a bowl. Make sure that it sits flat in the bottom of the pillowcase or bag.

Put heavy food, like potatoes, at the bottom, and lighter food, like peppers, at the top.

When securing the top of the pantry, make sure you leave enough rope to tie it to a branch.

Tie the pantry to a branch with two round turns and two half-hitch knots. Pull the rope tight.

How to make a camp shower using a thick plastic bag

Hang the plastic bag over a branch. Make sure the bag doesn't have any holes in it.

Fill a bottle with clean water. Now pour the water from the bottle into the plastic bag.

Using a sharp fork or penknife, carefully prick holes along the bottom of the plastic bag.

Quickly jump under the shower before all the water drains out! Fill it up again if you need to.

Keeping drinks cool

You can keep drinks cool by wrapping them in a damp cloth and placing them in a bowl of water in a shady spot. The water in the bowl will keep the cloth wet, which in turn will keep the drinks cool.

Try this with water and fruit juice.

1 Fill the bowl with cold water. Soak the dish towel in the water and wring it out. Wrap the dish towel around the bottles that you want to keep cool.

Make sure the bottle tops are closed tightly.

Thick dish towels soak up more water.

Plastic bowls do not heat up as quickly as metal bowls.

Cover as much of the bottles as you can.

2 Tuck the dish towel between the bottles. This will keep them cool longer, and will also stop the dish towel from slipping down.

Deep bowls will cover more of the bottles.

Make sure the bottom of the bowl is large enough to hold all the bottles.

3 Carefully lift the wrapped bottles into the bowl. Keep the bowl in a shady place. When the water in the bowl warms up, replace it with fresh cold water. If the dish towel has dried out, do not forget to soak it again.

Storing garbage

Burn all the garbage that you can, such as paper. Everything else must be stored and carried away with you. You should always leave your camp as if no one had ever been there.

Wrap garbage securely so that you can carry it home in your backpack.

Remember to collect all the garbage around your fire.

Crush boxes so that they take up less room.

⭐ Wrap paper and cardboard around sharp edges like the tops of cans.

Heat cans over your fire to burn off any food that might go bad or attract animals.

Carefully crush burned cans so they take up less room.

Sleeping outdoors

It can get very cold at night, so it is important to maintain your body heat and keep warm. Most of your body heat is lost from your head. The ground can also steal warmth. Putting layers between you and the ground and covering your head will help keep you warm and insulated.

In hot weather, sleep in a sheet bag rather than a sleeping bag.

Materials

T-shirt   String
Garbage bags

Newspaper

Soft sweater
Thread   Safety pin
Needle

Sheet

Blanket

Hints and tips

Most of your body heat is lost from your head and shoulders, so wear a hat on cold nights and pull your sleeping bag up over your head.

Make sure you keep your sleeping equipment dry; if it gets wet, it will not keep you warm.

Making a sleeping mat

You need to make a thick mat so that when you lie on it, you are far enough off the ground to be insulated.

1 Fill a garbage bag with crumpled newspaper. Squeeze the air out of the garbage bag and tie some string around the top. Secure the string with a reef knot.

 See page 54 to tie a reef knot.

2 To make your mat waterproof, slide the filled garbage bag inside another garbage bag. Tie a piece of string around the top of this garbage bag and secure the string with a reef knot.

Use thick garbage bags so they will not split easily.

Slide the knotted end into the second garbage bag first.

Make sure the blanket is big enough to cover all the bags.

You may need to fill two to three garbage bags depending on your height.

3 Lay the garbage bags end to end. Put a blanket over the top for extra comfort. When you sleep on your mat, the newspaper will absorb cold from the ground and keep you warm.

How to make a camp pillow with the T-shirt and the soft sweater

Lay the soft sweater out flat. Fold the sleeves in at the back and fold it in half.

Slide the folded sweater inside the T-shirt to make your camp pillow feel comfortable.

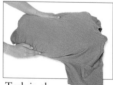

Tuck in the loose edges of the T-shirt and smooth away any bumps.

Making a sheet bag

A sheet bag helps you stay warm at night and keeps your sleeping bag clean and dry.

Use an old sheet so that you can cut the end if it is too long.

1 Fold a single sheet in half lengthwise. Make sure the sheet is long enough to cover your body and pull over your head.

How to make a drawstring for your sheet bag

Make a fold in the top edge of the sheet about 1 in (3 cm) deep to make room for the drawstring.

2 Sew up the side and bottom of the sheet with two rows of stitches. The inside row needs small, neat stitches because this is where the sheet will pull the most.

⚠ Be careful not to prick yourself with the needle.

Use strong thread to sew your sheet bag.

⚠ Running stitch is sewn in a straight line. The stitches and spaces between them are all the same length.

Sew two rows of stitches. Use small running stitches on the inside row. The outside ones can be larger.

🪢 See page 55 to tie a half-hitch knot.

3 Follow the instructions for adding the drawstring. Tie half-hitch knots in the ends of the string so that it does not slide back through the folded sheet.

Attach a safety pin to a piece of string and use it to guide the string through the folded sheet.

When it is cold, pull the sheet bag over your head.

Pull the draw-string and tie it inside your sheet bag.

⚠ Do not forget to remove the safety pin before using your sheet bag.

Buying sleeping equipment

Sleeping equipment varies depending on what you want to use it for. For example, sleeping bags can be made out of natural or artificial fibers. Natural-fiber sleeping bags will keep you very warm; artificial-fiber sleeping bags will dry out easily if they get wet.

A sweatshirt and pants will keep you warm at night.

Buy a sleeping bag with a drawstring hood to insulate your head.

Choose a large, foam sleeping mat since an inflatable one will puncture easily.

The zipper should be well insulated so it will not feel cold at night.

A curved back helps keep body heat around your head, neck, and shoulders.

Making a fire

Fires are very useful. They will keep you warm and enable you to cook food outdoors. However, unless watched at all times, they can spread easily and become dangerous. Always collect all the materials you need to make a fire first, so that you do not have to leave the fire once it is lit.

It is important to find dry wood for making your fire.

Materials

Dry grass   *Matches*

Dry leaves

Small sticks

Medium-sized sticks

Thick sticks

A tepee fire

This kind of fire is very easy to make and can be used in most conditions. Choose a spot well away from anything that might catch fire.

1 Ask an adult to help you remove a square of turf. Put the turf to the side. Now lay thick sticks in the hole, side by side.

The kindling should be bone dry.

2 Place some kindling on top of the thick sticks. Use small sticks the thickness of pencils, and small leaves. Build a tepee shape around the kindling with thinner sticks.

Leave a gap in the front to add the tinder.

3 Put some tinder inside the kindling. Use dry grass, dead leaves, fungus, or bark as your tinder. Now light the tinder with a match.

⭐ If you have never lit a fire before, ask an adult to help you.

Use a ball of tinder the size of a grapefruit.

More details on how to make a fire outdoors

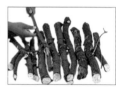

Find dry sticks that are about 2½ in (5 cm) around. Place them close together, side by side.

Use a good amount of kindling. Do not pack it together or it will not burn very well.

Balance the dry sticks against each other, with thicker, longer sticks on the outside.

Carefully light the tinder with a match. This will in turn light the kindling and the sticks.

Always watch your fire, making sure it does not burn too fiercely.

4 Once your fire is lit, it will burn fiercely. The tepee will collapse into a pile of very hot, flaming embers. When this happens, very carefully add more sticks. Thin sticks are best for cooking, and thick sticks are best for slow-burning fires to sit around.

Have extra fuel handy.

How to put out a fire safely using water, sand, or earth

Once the fire has died down, pour water over it. You could use dirty washing-up water.

You could also sprinkle sand or earth over the fire until it stops smoking.

5 When you have finished using your fire, always put it out – see above right. Carefully stir the embers with your foot to make sure there is nothing still burning.

Keep water or sand nearby in case you need to put out your fire quickly.

In some areas, it is forbidden to make a fire, so always check before you make one.

When the fire is cold, scrape the embers with a stick until they have all crumbled into ash.

Make sure you do not leave any garbage around the fire that could harm an animal.

Always replace the turf you cut out for your fire when leaving your camp.

Keep your feet away from a burning fire.

Be very careful when stirring the embers; they could be extremely hot.

What you need for a fire

The secret of a good fire is to start off with very small sticks and gradually add larger sticks as the fire gets going.

Tinder
This is the most important part of the fire – you cannot start a fire by lighting thick sticks.

Add to the tinder.

Kindling
When these tiny sticks burn, they set fire to the small fuel.

Small fuel
When this is alight, you have a fully burning fire.

Finger-thick sticks.

Main fuel
Once the fire is burning fully, add the main fuel to keep it going.

Break the sticks into 12-in (30-cm) pieces.

Large fuel
Logs are used for long-burning fires and semi-permanent camps.

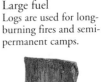

Logs must be burned completely before putting out a fire.

Cooking on a fire

Campfires get much hotter than kitchen stoves, so you must be very careful when you cook food on them. Always wait until the flames have died down slightly and the embers are glowing. If the fire cools down too much, you can always heat it up again by adding more sticks.

Smoke from the campfire will give your food a tasty smoked flavor.

Materials

Foil

Penknife

Twigs *String*

Branches

Hints and tips

Whenever you cook food, it is safest to lift the tripod and pot on and off the fire together.

Use finger-thick sticks to cook with so that you can control the cooking temperature.

Using a tripod

Always use a tripod placed over the fire when cooking.

Details on how to make a tripod and pot hook for cooking food

1 Wrap string around three sticks. Secure the string with a reef knot.

Try to find sticks that are about 3 ft (1 m) long.

See page 54 to tie a reef knot.

2 Spread the sticks out to form the tripod. Use a branch with strong twigs to make a pot hook. Strip off its leaves with a penknife.

See page 52 to learn how to use a penknife safely.

Make sure you do not wrap the string so tightly that you cannot spread out the tripod legs.

Make sure the string used to attach the pot hook is strong enough to support a pot full of water.

Hang the pot on different branches depending on how close to the fire you want it.

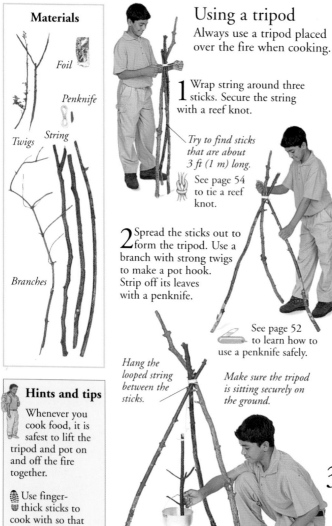

Hang the looped string between the sticks.

Make sure the tripod is sitting securely on the ground.

Hang the pot handle on one of the hook branches.

3 Wrap one end of a piece of string around the top of the pot hook and tie a reef knot in the string. Make a loop in the other end of the string and secure it with a reef knot. Now hang your pot hook on the tripod.

How to make useful cooking utensils with sticks and foil

Make a toasting fork by stripping the bark of a Y-shaped branch and shaving the ends into a point.

Strip a long, thin branch and shave the end into a point to make a skewer for cooking kabobs on.

Make a frying pan by wrapping foil around a Y-shaped branch. Squash the foil together.

See page 52 to learn how to use a penknife safely.

Different ways of cooking

One of the best things about cooking on a fire is that you can experiment with different cooking techniques. You need a few sticks, a penknife, and some foil.

Cooking sausages

Campfires get very hot and cook food quickly on the outside, but take longer to cook the inside. When cooking meat, it is especially important to make sure it is cooked all the way through. If it is not, you could get food poisoning.

Cut the meat into small pieces so that it cooks faster.

Thread thin sticks through the sausages and put them on a Y-shaped branch.

Making meat kabobs

Cut tomatoes, mushrooms, and fresh chicken into small pieces, and slide them onto the skewer. Cook the kabob for twenty minutes, until the meat is cooked.

Cook the kabobs on the grill made on page 32.

Cooking food over a fire with sticks and foil

Toast two slices of bread at the same time by putting them onto the sharpened Y-shaped stick.

Chop up vegetables and slide them onto the skewer, then cook them over your fire.

Cook fish on the frying pan. It is ready when the flesh turns white and the eyes cloud over.

Make sure you do not prick yourself on the sharp points.

Alternative cooking methods

Bacon in a paper bag
Poke a stick through the rolled top of a bag and hold the stick over a fire for 10 minutes. The bacon fat stops the bag from burning.

Burgers in leaves
If you do not have any foil, cook your burger in a cabbage or lettuce leaf instead. This will keep ashes out of the burger.

Egg in moss
Carefully prick the egg with a pin. Wrap the egg in moss and place it in the embers of a fire for a few minutes.

All-in-one stew

When you are outdoors, you will probably be very busy during the day, so it is important to eat a hot meal and have a hot drink in the evening. The hot drink will warm you up, and your body will be able to digest the food while you are sleeping, which will give you energy for the next day.

Always find the time to make a hot, filling meal every day.

Materials

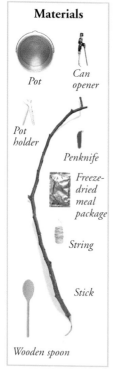

Pot

Can opener

Pot holder

Penknife

Freeze-dried meal package

String

Stick

Wooden spoon

Hints and tips

Take herbs, spices, curry powder, salt, and pepper with you; they will add a lot of flavor to your food.

Always eat everything that you cook; leftover food may attract animals to your camp.

All-in-one stew

This meal is very easy to make; just add your favorite ingredients to a store-bought freeze-dried meal package.

The package will tell you how much water to add.

 See page 52 to learn how to use a penknife safely.

1 Soak the freeze-dried food in your pot for one hour.

Mushrooms

Can of tomatoes

Dried fruit

Add anything you like, even fruit cake!

Zucchini

Tomato puree

2 When the dried food has absorbed the water, or rehydrated, add all the ingredients (see the detailed instructions, right). Stir everything together and hang the pot on a tripod over your fire.

See page 26 to make a tripod.

3 Let the stew simmer gently for one hour. When it is ready, take the stew off the fire and allow it to cool for a few minutes before serving; this will stop you from burning your tongue!

More details on how to make the all-in-one stew

Using a penknife, carefully slice one onion and a clove of garlic into small pieces.

Open the can of tomatoes with the can opener. Make sure you do not touch the sharp, cut edge.

Crumble a bouillon cube into the stew to give it extra flavor and to help thicken the stew.

Cut your vegetables into small pieces so they will cook quickly, and add them to the stew.

How to adapt your tripod to heat water safely

Wrap a piece of string around two of the tripod legs. Secure each end of the string with a reef knot.

Find a stick about 3 ft (1 m) long and lodge it between the sticks at the top of the tripod.

Wrap some string around one tripod leg and the stick. Secure the string with half-hitch knots at each end.

Hang the pot on the stick by its handle. A stick with a strong twig at the end is ideal.

How to heat water safely

It is very easy to scald yourself with hot liquids, so always be extra careful when heating water over a fire. Adapt a tripod so that you can heat water safely over your campfire.

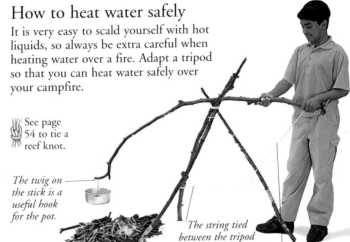

See page 54 to tie a reef knot.

The twig on the stick is a useful hook for the pot.

The string tied between the tripod legs makes the tripod more stable.

The string tied between the stick and tripod leg helps you use the stick as a lever.

1 To adapt your tripod, follow the detailed instructions, left. Half-fill the pot with water and hang it from the stick. Now lever the stick and pot over the fire.

See page 55 to tie a half-hitch knot.

2 When the water starts to produce steam, carefully lever the tripod away from the fire. Using a thick dish towel, carefully lift the pot off the stick.

Hold the stick firmly when you are moving it so that you have full control.

If you do not have a dish towel, use anything that will absorb heat and protect you.

⭐ If you feel unsure about levering the water on and off the fire, ask an adult to help you.

Hot drinks

When making hot drinks outdoors, the water does not need to be boiling hot; boiling water can scald you, and will be too hot to drink.

⭐ Always let any steam from the water die down before pouring into a mug.

1 If you are making a package drink with a dairy product in it, mix it into a paste with cold water first.

2 Hold the pot of water with a dish towel. Carefully pour the water away from you into the mug.

3 Stir your drink to get rid of any lumps. Store it in a thermos if you want to save it for later.

More recipe ideas

When cooking outdoors, the main thing to remember is that some foods take longer to cook than others, so you have to plan ahead when preparing a meal. For example, you would need to prepare baked potatoes and put them in the embers of your fire long before grilling a fish.

Experiment with lots of different camp recipes for exciting meals.

Materials

Wooden spoon

Fork

Penknife

Foil

Stick

Pot

Bowl

Damper bread

This traditional Australian campfire meal is very quick and easy to make.

1 Mix some flour and water. Add the water a little at a time until it turns the flour into a dough.

Mix the dough in a pot or bowl.

2 Keep your hands straight and roll the dough in between them to make a sausage shape. If the dough starts to feel sticky, add more flour to it.

See page 26 to make a tripod and pot hook.

3 Wrap the dough around the stick in a spiral and place it on a grill (see page 31.) When the bread is cooked, it will look golden brown and will slide off the stick easily.

Make a tight spiral shape.

How to prepare vegetables to cook over a campfire

Wash the vegetables thoroughly in clean water to get rid of any soil.

Using your penknife or another knife, carefully slice the vegetables into small pieces.

Put the vegetables in a pot of cold water. Hang the pot on the pot hook attached to the tripod.

Cook the vegetables in boiling water for about 10 minutes. Check if they are done with a knife.

Hints and tips

If you cook meat over the grill, watch out for meat fat dripping into the fire; the fat will make the fire hotter.

Always take your pot off the fire and wait for the steam to die down before testing your food.

How to prepare a potato for baking in the embers

Wash the potato, and then prick it all over with a fork to stop the skin from splitting when it cooks.

Rub butter and salt on the potato. This will make the potato skin crisp and full of flavor.

Wrap the potato in foil and place it in the embers of the fire. Leave it to cook for one hour.

See page 52 to learn how to use a penknife safely.

Grilling fish

The best way to cook fresh fish when you are outdoors is on a grill placed over a campfire.

See page 32 to make a grill.

1 Place the fish on the grill and then carefully lift the grill and tripod over a fire.

See page 24 to make a fire.

If the tripod feels heavy, ask an adult to help you.

Make sure the flames of the fire have died down slightly before you start cooking on it.

2 Watch the fish while it is cooking over the fire. If the fire is not hot enough, add a few more sticks.

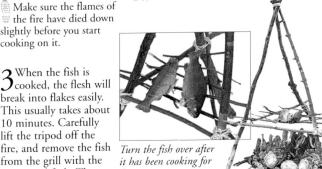

Turn the fish over after it has been cooking for five minutes.

3 When the fish is cooked, the flesh will break into flakes easily. This usually takes about 10 minutes. Carefully lift the tripod off the fire, and remove the fish from the grill with the spoon and fork. The fish will crumble easily.

Food through the day

When you are outdoors, it is important to eat and drink regularly. Eat snacks throughout the day to give you energy. Have your main meal in the evening.

Dried fruit and nuts

Candy provides lots of energy.

Cookies

Baked potato

All-in-one meal

Hot drink

Apple

Orange

Water

Cereal

Fruit juice

Chocolate

Breakfast
Always eat a filling breakfast and have plenty to drink. Porridge is ideal on cold days.

Lunch
Choose food that is easy to carry, like sandwiches and granola bars. Pack sweet foods for extra energy.

Dinner
Cook something hot and filling. Use any remaining heat from the fire to make a hot bedtime drink.

Making camp equipment

Some pieces of camp equipment, such as a stool or cooking grill, are very useful, but bulky and heavy to carry around. If you know how to make them from natural materials, you will have less to take with you. Once you have made the equipment shown on these pages, experiment and make other useful items.

Simple camp equipment will make your camp more comfortable.

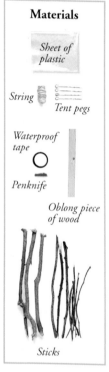

Materials

Sheet of plastic

String *Tent pegs*

Waterproof tape

Penknife

Oblong piece of wood

Sticks

Hints and tips

Flatten the tops of the sticks on the camp stool to make the stool more comfortable to sit on.

Keep your mud scraper close to your tent so that you remember to clean your boots before going inside your tent.

Making a grill

Adapt the tripod shown on page 26 to make a grill to cook food on over your campfire.

1 Tie, or lash, three sticks to the tripod base using square lashing (see the detailed instructions, right).

See page 57 to tie square lashing.

You could also use this grill to dry food on.

Try to find sticks about 1½ ft (50 cm) long.

2 Use the three sticks lashed to the tripod as a base to lay smaller sticks across. The smaller sticks will form the grill.

Break the sticks to the correct length.

3 Lay the sticks side by side, close together. Use small green sticks – they will not catch fire very easily.

Cook fish, damper bread, and kabobs on the grill.

More details on how to adapt the tripod to make a grill

Take one of the sticks and lash one end to one of the tripod legs about 1½ ft (50 cm) from the bottom.

Lash the other end of the stick onto another tripod leg. Repeat with the other two sticks.

Try to find straight sticks to lay across because bent ones will not support your food very well.

Make a crisscross pattern with the sticks if you are cooking small pieces of food.

How to make the seat of the camp stool with plastic and tape

Wrap string around the top of each stick so that it will support the seat of the camp stool.

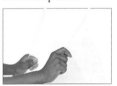

Fold the sheet of plastic to make a triangular shape and then fold it over again.

Seal the open edges of the plastic sheet with some strong waterproof tape.

Using a penknife, carefully slice a hole through one layer of the plastic sheet in each corner.

Making a camp stool

You only need to pack the seat of the stool; you can make the legs when you need them.

1 Take three strong sticks about 3 ft (1 m) long and lash them together with string. Wrap the string around the legs several times and then secure the string with a reef knot. Now spread the legs out.

See page 54 to tie a reef knot.

Spread the legs out.

Make sure the tops of the sticks are pushed out as far as they will go.

2 Wrap a piece of string around the top of one of the legs. Secure the string with a reef knot. Now wrap it around the top of the second leg and tie a half-hitch knot in the string. Repeat on the third leg. Wrap the string back around the first leg and secure it with another reef knot.

See page 55 to tie a half-hitch knot.

Push the top of the leg into the cut plastic sheet.

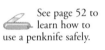

See page 52 to learn how to use a penknife safely.

3 Place the plastic seat of the camp stool over the tripod legs. Make sure that the three holes in the seat slot over the three tripod legs. This will keep the seat secure when you sit on it.

Making a mud scraper

Keep your boots clean by making a mud scraper for your camp.

1 Find an oblong piece of wood. The top needs to be thin so that you can scrape your boots along it.

2 Push four tent pegs, two on each side, into the ground to hold the wood upright. You can use sticks instead of tent pegs.

3 Scrape the bottom of your boot along the top of the mud scraper to remove any mud.

Water in your camp

Collecting water is a vital job outdoors; you will need it for drinking, cooking, and cleaning up. Apart from rainwater collected directly from the sky, you cannot guarantee that the water you collect will be clean, or sterile, so you must learn the techniques shown here to be sure you always have clean water.

One way of ensuring the water you collect is safe to drink is to boil it.

Materials

Water bottle

Clean sock

String

Ground sheet

Sticks

Stones

Hints and tips

Leave water that you want to sterilize to stand overnight so that any sediment can settle.

It is important to have a constant supply of fresh water. If it is very hot, or you are going on a long trip, pack several water bottles.

Sterilizing water

Follow the instructions below if you do not have sterilizing tablets with you.

See page 26 to make a pot hook and tripod.

1 Hang the sock on the pot hook and place a bowl underneath it. Now filter the water by pouring it through the sock and into the bowl.

2 When the water has filtered through the sock and into the bowl, pour the water into your pot.

3 Hang the pot on the pot hook. Carefully lift the tripod over a lit fire. Leave the water to boil for at least two minutes. When the fire has died down and the water has cooled, lift the tripod off the fire. You can now pour the sterilized water into a water container.

Cleaning water using a sterilizing tablet

Put the sterilizing tablet in the water bottle. You will need one tablet for each pint (half liter) of water.

Let the water stand for one hour. The sterilizing tablet will dissolve and clean the water.

⭐ If the tripod feels heavy, ask an adult to help you.

Making a water collector

Rainwater is the cleanest natural water. Collect it as it falls using this water collector.

The sticks will lift the ground sheet off the ground.

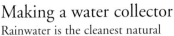

1 Lay the ground sheet out flat. Make a small hole in the middle of one side. Tie a piece of string to this hole and tie the other end around a heavy stone (see the detailed instructions, right).

Attach heavy stones with string to each corner of the ground sheet.

Make the hole on the front edge.

Use longer sticks at the back.

Use shorter sticks at the front.

2 Use the sticks to lift the corners of the ground sheet off the ground. Move the stones outward so that they pull the sticks upright.

See far right to shorten the string.

This hole should not have a stick pushed through it.

The longer sticks make the water run down the ground sheet.

Collect the rainwater as soon as it has fallen.

3 Continue adjusting the stones until the sticks are standing upright. Place the bowl under the hole in the ground sheet at the front to collect the rainwater.

The weight of the stone will make the ground sheet dip in the middle.

More details on how to make your water collector

Thread the string through each hole and secure the string with a half-hitch knot.

Wrap the string around the stone once. Tie a reef knot in the string to secure it to the stone.

Push each stick through each hole in the ground sheet, taking care not to make the holes larger.

Shorten the string by wrapping it around the stone until it is the correct length.

See page 54 to tie a reef knot, and page 55 to tie a half-hitch knot.

Storing water

Once you have collected your water and sterilized it, you will need to store it. Keep most of your water in a large container in the shade. When you are out walking, use a water bottle to store your water. Do not store anything else in these containers, and clean them regularly.

Collapsible water containers are easy to pack in your backpack.

Choose a water bottle with a clip so that you can clip it onto your belt.

Using a compass

One of your most important pieces of equipment is your compass. It will help you navigate, or find your way, so that you can hike through unmarked terrain and find a specific destination. If you do not have your own compass, you can make one by following the instructions on page 37.

A compass will help you navigate when you are outdoors.

Materials

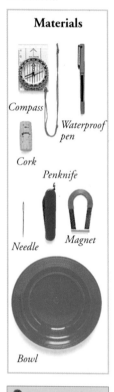

Compass

Waterproof pen

Cork

Penknife

Needle

Magnet

Bowl

Hints and tips

A circle has 360 degrees (°). Moving clockwise, north is at 0°, east is at 90°, south is at 180°, and west is at 270°.

Use the cord on your compass to hang it around your neck so it is always handy whenever you need to use it.

Getting your bearings

Bearings are used to tell direction. You can use your compass to find the exact direction of an object by taking its bearing.

1 Put the compass on a firm, flat surface. When taking bearings, always keep the compass in the same place and swivel it around.

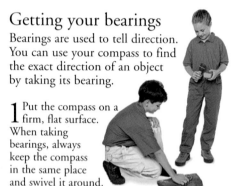

2 Place the objects around the compass. Look at the labeled compass on page 37 to see what the different parts are called.

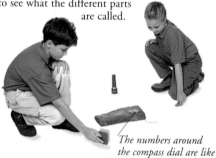

The numbers around the compass dial are like the degrees in a circle.

Practice taking bearings with different objects.

3 Point the direction arrow at the first object. Turn the compass dial around so that the blue arrow sits on top of the red north arrow. Follow the instructions, right, to read the bearing.

This bearing is 250°, which is approximately west.

More details on how to find bearings with a compass

The compass has a magnet in it, so make sure you do not put it near anything made of metal.

Swivel the compass so that the direction arrow is pointing toward the first object.

The blue arrow shows you where north is in relation to the object that you are looking at.

The base of the direction arrow lines up with a number on the compass dial. This is the bearing

How to magnetize a needle so that it points north

With the eye, or hole, of the needle pointing downward, stroke the magnet along the needle.

Make sure you always stroke the magnet down the needle. This will magnetize the needle.

Using a penknife, carefully slice a piece of cork. Now follow the instructions, right.

See page 52 to learn how to use a penknife safely.

Making your own compass

There are various ways to tell direction. The easiest way is to use the Earth's own magnetic field. A magnetized needle works like a compass, swinging around to always point to magnetic north.

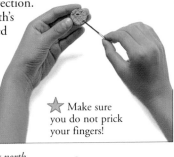

1 Carefully push the point of the magnetized needle through the sliced cork. If the cork is too hard, ask an adult to help you.

⭐ Make sure you do not prick your fingers!

Point of the needle

Arrow showing north

East

West

Eye of the needle

South

🖊 Use a waterproof pen so that the ink will not run in the water.

2 Draw an arrow on the cork toward the point of the needle. This is your north point. Draw dots around the cork to show east, south, and west.

3 Half-fill a bowl with water and place it on a flat surface. Float the cork on the water. When the water has settled, the point of the needle will swing around to point north.

🖊 Use a compass to double-check that the point of the needle is pointing north.

Protractor compass

You can find directions and take bearings with this kind of compass.

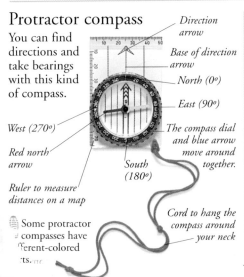

Direction arrow

Base of direction arrow

North (0°)

East (90°)

The compass dial and blue arrow move around together.

West (270°)

Red north arrow

Ruler to measure distances on a map

South (180°)

Cord to hang the compass around your neck

🖊 Some protractor compasses have different-colored points.

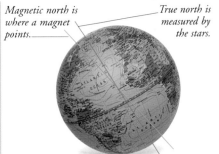

Magnetic north is where a magnet points.

True north is measured by the stars.

Where is north?

There are three different kinds of north. True north is found using the stars, and magnetic north is where a compass needle points. Grid north is only marked on maps and map grid lines. It is in between true north and magnetic north.

Reading a map

A map shows the position of an object and what the land, or terrain, is like. To use a map, look around you for landmarks, such as roads, rivers, or forests. Turn the map around until the landmarks on the map line up with the landmarks you can see. This will help you figure out exactly where you are.

Learn how to read a map so that you can navigate anywhere.

Materials

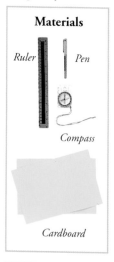

Ruler　　　*Pen*

Compass

Cardboard

The parts of a map

All maps are covered in symbols that represent the landmarks in the area. Look for a panel called a legend (see below) that explains what all the symbols mean.

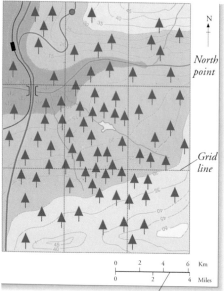

N↑
North point

Grid line

Distance is represented by a scale bar. Here 1 in = 1.2 miles (2 cm = 2 km).

Contour, three-dimensional, street, and underground maps

On contour maps, the colored lines join points of equal height, showing how the land slopes.

This three-dimensional map covers a small area in great detail, making it ideal for walking trips.

Street maps are used in built-up areas where you may need to get to your destination by road.

This section of a subway map is not drawn to scale. It shows where all the stations are.

Hints and tips

Grid lines are always spaced at equal distances on a map. If you know how much the distance between each grid line represents, you can figure out distances on maps very quickly.

The upright, or vertical, grid lines on a map always point north.

Steep hills are shown on maps by lots of contour lines close together. On gentler slopes, the contour lines are farther apart.

Legend

The symbols below form the legend for the map above. Study the symbols so that you can understand the map.

● *Town*

Road

■ *Train station*

Railroad line

Woodland

—40— *Contour line*

River

Lake

Marshland

Bridge

Details on how to make a map of your area

To make the grid, draw straight lines across and down the page at 1½-in (4-cm) intervals

Keeping the compass on the cross, swivel it so that the compass is pointing toward the first object.

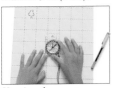

Put a dot by the direction arrow. Lay your ruler along the cross and this dot and measure 3 in (8 cm).

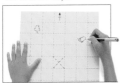

Keeping the compass over the cross, point the direction arrow toward the second object.

Continue adding objects until the map has got all the details you need to represent the area.

Remember to add a scale bar and legend to your map.

How to make a map

Follow these instructions to make your own map so that you can record your surroundings.

See page 37 to learn the parts of a compass.

1 Draw a grid and put a north arrow parallel to the upright, or vertical, grid lines, and a cross in the middle of the page. Put the compass over the cross and turn the map until the vertical grid lines align with the red north arrow on the compass.

Draw objects all around you; not just in front of you.

For accurate steps, place the heel of your front foot up against the toes of your back foot.

2 With the direction arrow pointing toward the first object you want to record, ask a friend to take tiny steps toward it. Make sure she counts the number of steps she takes.

Use several tree symbols close together to represent a forest.

3 Make your scale five tiny steps to 1½ in (4 cm). If your friend took 10 tiny steps to reach the object, you would need to measure 3 in (8 cm) along the ruler (see the detailed instructions, left).

To make the scale more accurate, measure your friend's feet. If they are 8 in (20 cm) long, you can say that for every five 8-in (20-cm) steps taken, you will measure 1½ in (4 cm) on the map.

Choose landmarks that are easy to recognize from a distance.

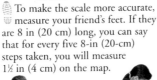

Make sure your friend walks in a straight line.

4 Now ask your friend to walk toward the second object and repeat what you did for the first object. Make sure she always starts walking from where you are sitting.

Finding your way

If you can use a map and compass together, you should be able to figure out exactly where you are and how to get to your destination. A route card is also very useful. You can use it to determine how long it will take you to walk to your destination, and you can make notes on it about what to look for along your walk.

Protect your map by keeping it in a waterproof map case.

Materials

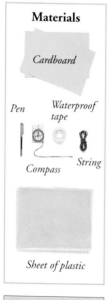

Cardboard

Pen   Waterproof tape

Compass   String

Sheet of plastic

Hints and tips

Before setting off on a walking trip, always tell someone where you are going and when you expect to be back.

On level ground, you can expect to walk about three miles (five kilometers) an hour. Allow longer if you are walking uphill or on uneven ground.

Remember to take a new bearing every thirty minutes.

Making a route card

Mark your route on a piece of cardboard following the instructions below.

1 Place the corner of the cardboard next to your starting point. Here, it is the train station. Draw a line down from this point, and a symbol to represent the station.

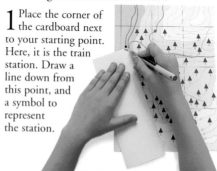

2 Pivot the cardboard so it aligns with the next point on your route. If the path does not follow a straight line, align the cardboard to the first point where the path bends. Mark this point and follow the detailed instructions, top right.

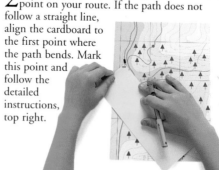

3 When you have marked all the points of your route, align the edge of the cardboard with the scale bar on your map. Divide the route into one-mile sections.

More details on how to make a route card for a walking trip

Pivot the cardboard so that the previous point and the new point to be marked are aligned.

If your path crosses contour lines, indicating changes in land height, make a note of them.

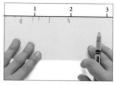

Using the scale bar, try to figure out how long your route will take you to walk.

Use your route card to make sure that you have not chosen a route that is too long.

Make a note of any interesting places that you may want to look at on your route.

How to make a map case with the sheet of plastic, string, and tape

Cut the plastic so that when it is folded in half, it will cover a folded map easily.

Fold the bottom of the plastic up and seal it with the waterproof tape. Make two holes in the sheet.

Thread the string through the two holes and secure each end with a half-hitch knot.

Now slide the map into the plastic. Fold over the top and seal it with waterproof tape.

The string enables you to hang the map case around your neck. Shorten it by tying a half-hitch knot.

 See page 55 to tie a half-hitch knot.

Using a compass, map, and route card

When you are walking in new places, check that you are going in the right direction by taking compass bearings regularly, using your map to help you find landmarks, and following your route card.

1 Put the compass over the point on the map that represents where you are standing.

See page 37 to learn the parts of a compass.

Blue direction arrow

Compass dial

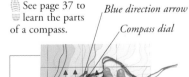

2 Keep the compass flat on the map and swivel the compass dial until the blue direction arrow is parallel to the grid lines pointing upward, or vertically.

Red north arrow

3 Turn the map until the red north arrow is sitting on top of the blue direction arrow. Now take a bearing of the point you want to walk to – the first point on your route card.

See page 36 to learn how to take bearings.

4 Turn to face the direction in which you are going to walk. Keep this point on the map ahead of you and use the compass to maintain the correct bearing. Make sure that the red north arrow and the blue direction arrow are always pointing in the same direction.

If you cannot reach your destination by walking in a straight line, take new bearings every time you make a detour.

Using the Sun and stars

Even without a map or compass, you can still navigate by using your natural sense of direction, the Sun, and the stars. Find out if you live in the northern or southern hemisphere and then follow the techniques shown on these pages to navigate when you are out walking.

Use natural signs and your own sense of direction to navigate.

Materials

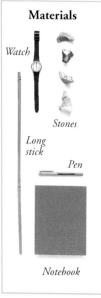

Watch

Stones

Long stick

Pen

Notebook

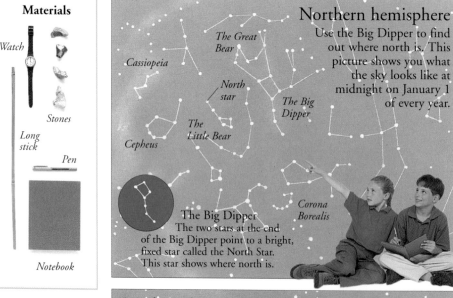

Northern hemisphere

Use the Big Dipper to find out where north is. This picture shows you what the sky looks like at midnight on January 1 of every year.

The Great Bear

Cassiopeia

North star

The Big Dipper

The Little Bear

Cepheus

Corona Borealis

The Big Dipper
The two stars at the end of the Big Dipper point to a bright, fixed star called the North Star. This star shows where north is.

Hints and tips

A constellation is a group of stars. The Southern Cross and Great Bear are both constellations.

🐾 The seven stars that form the tail and rump of the Great Bear are known as the Big Dipper.

🐾 The Southern Cross is in the misty band of stars called the Milky Way.

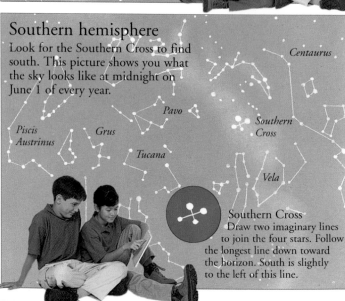

Southern hemisphere

Look for the Southern Cross to find south. This picture shows you what the sky looks like at midnight on June 1 of every year.

Centaurus

Pavo

Piscis Austrinus

Grus

Southern Cross

Tucana

Vela

Southern Cross
Draw two imaginary lines to join the four stars. Follow the longest line down toward the horizon. South is slightly to the left of this line.

Navigating with the Sun

The Sun always rises in the east and sets in the west, so you can use it to figure out where you are. By making a sundial, you will be able to use the Sun to find directions.

Push the stick firmly into the ground.

1 In the early morning, push a stick into the ground. A shadow will form on the side opposite the Sun. Mark the end of the shadow with a stone. The shadow will be pointing west since the Sun has risen in the east.

How to figure out where east, west, north, and south are

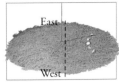

East

West

Using the east–west line you drew from the Sun's shadow, face east. North will be on your left.

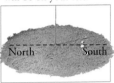

North   South

South will be on your right. This is because south is always directly opposite north.

Use a straight stick so that it forms a straight shadow.

2 Use the stones to mark the position of the shadow at intervals through the day. In the afternoon, the Sun will move toward the west, and its shadow will point toward the east.

The Sun's shadow creates a curve through the day as the Sun moves across the sky.

The closer you are to the Equator, the shorter your shadow will be. This is because the Sun passes directly overhead at the equator.

Line that runs east–west

3 Late in the afternoon, draw a straight line between the stones that you have been putting down. This line will point exactly east–west. Now draw a line at right angles to this line and straight through the base of the stick. This new line runs north–south.

Line that runs north–south

Finding direction with your watch

By using your watch and the Sun, you can figure out where north and south are very accurately.

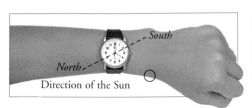

South

North

Direction of the Sun

Direction of the Sun

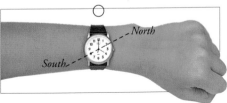

North

South

In the northern hemisphere
Point the hour hand at the Sun. South lies halfway between the hour hand and the 12 o'clock position.

In the southern hemisphere
Point the 12 o'clock position at the Sun. North lies halfway between this and the position of the hour hand.

Messages and trails

Sending messages and laying trails are important and useful outdoor skills. They enable you to let others know what you are doing and if you need anything. If you go hiking without a map, you must leave a trail so that other people know where you have gone, and so you can find your way back.

Use natural materials to lay trails that only your friends can recognize.

Materials

Assorted leaves

Twigs and branches

Grasses

Stones and pebbles

Hints and tips

- Use leaves, twigs, and branches that have already fallen to the ground.
- Make the first signs easy to recognize, and later signs harder.
- Write down flag signals as they are being sent and decode them afterward.

Laying a trail

Use natural materials and change them in a way that only your friends will recognize, such as breaking a leaf or snapping a twig.

1 Before you start, make up a few standard signs, such as "turn left", "turn right", "go straight ahead", "take so many steps", and "no entry".

Do not forget to tell your friends what the signs mean before you set off!

Leave a "no entry" sign on a path you do not want your friends to follow.

Use signs together to make your instructions extra clear.

Use a sign to say "keep going".

2 If the path splits, make sure you leave very clear signs that say which path to take. Otherwise your friends may take the wrong path.

Use a "turn around" sign to make sure your friends do not go down the wrong path.

Signs you can make to lay on your trail

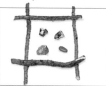

Make a square with four branches and put pebbles inside. Each pebble can represent one step.

Make an arrow with three branches or sticks. Point the arrow in the direction you are going.

Adapt the arrow sign to make a "turn around" sign by adding two more sticks or branches.

A cross usually means no, so this is a good sign to use when you want to say "no entry".

Signs you can make (continued)

Lay a stick on a Y-shaped twig. Put a leaf on the end of the stick to point to the path you have taken.

Tie a knot in a clump of grass. Point the top end in the direction you have gone.

Weave a twig into a leaf. This sign means "keep going". It is handy when the path is very long.

A leaf sandwiched between two pebbles or stones could mean "hidden treasure"!

This is a very useful sign. It means "go home". You could use stones, pebbles, or leaves.

Practice laying trails and making up signs before you go off on an expedition.

3 Lay your trail to the side of the path so that the symbols are less likely to be disturbed. Make sure that your symbols stand out. If they do not, your friends could easily miss them.

Break a large stick into smaller pieces to make a "turn around" sign.

Turn leaves upside down to make the signs stand out more.

4 Make sure you lay a sign to show the trail has ended. If you do not, your friends will not know when to go home!

The knotted grass tells you to go straight.

Sending flag signals

Flag signals are a great way to send messages to your friends when they are a long way off. Choose movements that are easy to understand, and always send the signals slowly. It is much harder to receive signals than to send them.

Simple movements could represent letters or whole words.

Always have a signal to say "send again" and "we understand".

Stand where you can be seen easily.

Tie your flag onto a stick.

Plant watch

All plants like slightly different conditions. If you know the conditions the plants around you like, you can tell all kinds of things, including whether it is usually wet or dry, and which insects and animals may be around.

Even the bark of a tree can provide information on your surroundings.

Materials

Coloring crayons

Sketch-book

Magnify-ing glass

Pencils

Pens   *Flashlight*

Notebooks

🍃 Ecology box

Flowers die soon after they have been picked. To remember what they look like, draw them instead.

🍃 Plants grow toward the Sun. They grow toward the south in the northern hemisphere, and toward the north in the southern hemisphere.

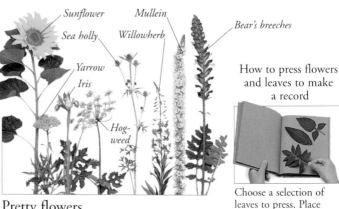

Sunflower — Mullein — Bear's breeches — Sea holly — Willowherb — Yarrow — Iris — Hog-weed

Pretty flowers

Most flowering plants need lots of water. If they are looking wilted and are drooping, it probably has not rained for a while.

Wheat heads

Most cacti like very hot, dry conditions.

Unusual flowers

Even grasses and cacti have flowers. The wheat shown above grows in many parts of the world.

No flowers

Mosses, ferns, and lichens do not flower. They all like damp conditions; mosses grow on the shady sides of rocks, hill slopes, and tree trunks, lichens grow on the sunny sides.

Ferns cluster on damp ground.

Moss

How to press flowers and leaves to make a record

Choose a selection of leaves to press. Place them inside a book on a sheet of blotting paper.

Leave enough room around the leaves to label them with their location.

Close the book and place a large stone on top of it. Leave it for several days to flatten the leaves.

Lichens grow only where the air is very clean.

Welcoming trees

A tree provides shelter and food for an amazing variety of animals. Owls sleep in holes in the trunk, hundreds of insects live among the leaves, and birds nest throughout the tree.

The clues that trees can provide

Deciduous trees drop their broad, flat leaves in the winter. They are common in warm places.

Coniferous trees have spiky, needlelike leaves. These trees often grow in cold places.

⭐ The fruits and seeds of some trees are poisonous.

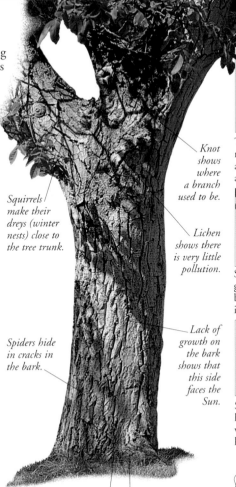

Squirrels make their dreys (winter nests) close to the tree trunk.

Spiders hide in cracks in the bark.

The trunk carries food down from the leaves to the roots.

Knot shows where a branch used to be.

Lichen shows there is very little pollution.

Lack of growth on the bark shows that this side faces the Sun.

The bark protects the tree's living tissues.

Different things you can find on trees

These brightly colored mountain ash berries attract hungy birds and animals.

Sometimes twigs will grow from a tree's trunk, but they will not grow into main branches.

Some fungi live in harmony with a tree, while others, such as honey fungus, destroy it.

When deciduous trees lose their leaves in the winter, you can identify them by their bark.

A tree's bark

If you do not know how old a tree is, studying its bark will give you some clues. The bark is the living part of the trunk, and it changes as the tree gets older.

Making a bark rubbing

Young bark is very smooth.

Old bark often has ridges and cracks.

Young bark is under the flaky old bark.

1 Keep a record of the trees in your area by taking rubbings of their bark. Make a note of each tree's name.

2 Place a piece of paper on the bark and gently rub a crayon over the top until you can see the pattern of the bark.

3 Note down the tree's name next to the rubbing. Take rubbings from other trees to build up your own tree record.

Animal watch

Wild animals are frightened of people and will usually hide from you. You can still tell they are around though, by studying all the signs they leave behind. Each species or kind of animal can be identified by its footprints. Droppings and dens can also give you a very good idea of what animals are in the vicinity.

Take a flashlight with you so that you can spot animals at night.

Materials

Magnifying glass

Pencils

Crayons

Flashlight

Pens

Tissues

Jar

Sketchbooks

Ecology box

Cobwebs are very fragile, so should not be touched.

Insects, particularly ants, usually follow the same track, which often leads to a source of food.

You should never remove anything from an animal's den.

Animal tracks

By studying tracks left in soft ground you can tell what animals have passed through.

How to identify different types of animal tracks

Paw prints

Hunting animals have paws, often with claws. By looking at the shape and size of the pads, you can identify which animal the track belongs to.

This is a footprint of a domestic dog. You can tell this from the size and shape of the pads.

Hoof prints

Grazing animals, such as sheep, goats, and deer, have hard, narrow feet called hooves. They can run very quickly from dangerous animals.

This sheep's hoof has two toes with a space in the middle. It is called a cloven hoof.

Hopping prints

Small birds, such as crows and sparrows, are very light and have feet that are designed to grasp branches, so they hop instead of walk.

The open-toed print of this crow shows that it is a perching bird. The back claw grips on to branches.

Wading prints

Large birds, like ducks and geese, waddle from side to side as they walk. Their toes have skin in between them, making their feet webbed.

The joined edge of this duck's foot shows it has webbed feet, allowing it to walk on wet ground.

What animals leave behind

Streamlined tail and wing feathers

Smooth body feathers

Warm down feather

Detecting signs of animal life around you

Spiders' webs are common everywhere. They are easiest to see in the morning dew.

Insects like sow bugs feed at night, so you will usually find their tracks in the morning.

Rabbits, like many other plant eaters, have rounded droppings that are very fibrous.

Birds leave rough-edged holes around nuts, whereas rodents leave tiny teeth marks.

Which feather?

There are many types of bird feathers: fluffy down feathers, smooth body feathers, and streamlined wing and tail feathers.

Sycamore leaf attacked by camber fungus showing it grew in polluted air

Tasty leaves

It's easy to tell when leaves have been attacked by caterpillars or fungi. Caterpillars leave just a skeleton of the leaf behind, and fungi leave black spots.

Cherry leaf eaten by a caterpillar

Gnawed food

Animals gnaw food in different ways, making it possible to tell which animals are around.

Hazelnut shells eaten by a vole

Pinecones stripped by a squirrel

Snail shells gnawed by a rat

Animal homes to look out for

Wasps' nests are made of chewed wood and hang from branches or holes in trees.

Many birds build cup-shaped nests in trees. They weave all sorts of things into their nests.

Some animals, like rabbits, sleep in burrows that they have dug underground.

Nocturnal animals

Unlike us, many animals are nocturnal: they sleep during the day and are awake at night. Nocturnal animals include foxes, raccoons, possums, gerbils, and moths. Follow the instructions below to attract moths at night so you can study them.

If you shine a bright light into the eyes of a nocturnal animal, it will be blinded and may not be able to move out of your way.

1 Loosely roll a light-colored tissue and slide it inside a jar. A clear jar is best, so the light can shine through it.

2 Place the jar on a firm, flat surface. Shine a flashlight inside the jar. Make sure it shines through the tissue.

3 Moths will soon be attracted to the lit tissue. Keep a record of the number and sizes of the moths that gather.

Weather watch

When you are outdoors, it is important to be able to predict the weather so that you are prepared for any changes. The wind brings changes in the weather, and you can predict these changes by studying the clouds. The size and shape of the clouds will tell you if it is going to be sunny or rainy.

Learning to predict the weather can keep you from getting caught in the rain!

Materials

Protractor

Small, light ball

Thread

Ruler   *Pebbles*

Scissors

Tape

Sheet of plastic

Waterproof tape

Pot

Bowl

Hints and tips

A clear sky in the evening can mean a very cold night. This is because there are not any clouds to keep the ground warm.

Insect-eating birds feed higher in good weather and lower when a storm is approaching.

Measuring wind speed

Changes in wind speed can indicate changes in the weather, so it is important to note what the wind is doing.

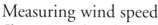

Tie about 1½ ft (50 cm) of thread in the middle of the bar.

1 Wrap some thread around the bar of the protractor. Secure the thread with a reef knot.

See page 54 to tie a reef knot.

2 Tape the other end of the thread to a small, light ball.

Use strong tape.

3 Hold the protractor upside down from the bar. When you hold the protractor parallel to the wind, you can read the angle the ball is blown to by the wind, and so determine the wind speed.

30° at 30 mph (50 kph)

60° at 15 mph (25 kph)

75° at 6 mph (10 kph)

90° at 0 mph (0 kph)

How clouds can help you predict the weather

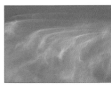

A cirrus cloud is high and wispy. It is made of ice crystals, and usually means fair weather.

A cirrocumulus cloud is small, white, and lumpy. It is found high up, and usually brings fair weather.

A cirrostratus cloud is a thin, hazy, white or gray sheet. When it thickens, rain may be on the way.

A stratocumulus cloud appears low down in the sky and can bring rain or light drizzle.

Using clouds to predict the weather (continued)

Altocumulus clouds are white or gray clumps, which may be separate or merged. They can mean fair weather.

A cumulus cloud appears in a blue sky in fine weather. It is white and puffy on top.

Cumulonimbus is a huge cumulus cloud, bringing showers of heavy rain and perhaps thunder.

Altostratus is a gray sheet-like cloud. If it starts getting thicker, rain may be on the way.

A hill-stratus cloud is a sheetlike cloud that covers hills. It produces fog high up in the hills.

High clouds indicate good weather, whereas lower clouds generally bring rain.

Making a rain gauge

When it rains, a lot of water is absorbed by the ground. This makes it difficult to figure out exactly how much rain has fallen. A rain gauge collects rain as it falls so you can measure it.

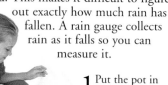

1 Put the pot in the bowl. Lay the cut plastic sheet over the top. The instructions to the right show you how to cut the sheet.

2 Fold the plastic sheet so that the cut section is over the pot and the rest of the sheet hangs over the top of the bowl. Secure the plastic sheet with the waterproof tape. Use the pebbles to weigh down the plastic sheet in the middle.

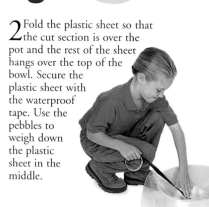

3 Tape the plastic sheet to the edge of the bowl. To figure out the rainfall, measure the widest part, or diameter, of the bowl and pot. The bowl used here is 12 ½ in (32 cm) in diameter, and the pot is 6 ¼ in (16 cm). Follow the instructions, right.

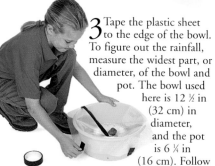

How to cut the sheet and measure the rainwater collected

Fold the plastic sheet in four and then carefully cut a tiny piece out of the folded corner.

Push the middle section of the plastic sheet into the pot. Fold and tape the sheet.

Divide the diameter of the bowl by the diameter of the pot. In this case it is 12 ½ ÷ 6 ¼ = 2.

Measure the depth of water in the pot. Here it is ½ in. Now multiply this number by the divided diameters. Here it is ½ x 2 = 1, so one inch of rain fell on every square inch of ground.

Natural weather signs

Many plants are very sensitive to changes in the weather.

In wet weather, a pine-cone will close up.

A pinecone will be open in dry weather.

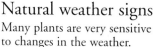

In dry weather, seaweed shrivels up and feels dry.

Seaweed swells and feels damp in wet weather.

Using a penknife safely

A good penknife will help you make all kinds of things and is therefore an important piece of your outdoor equipment. However, it can be dangerous, so you must learn how to use it safely. You need to know how to open and close it and keep it sharp, and how to cut with it.

If you have not used a penknife before, ask an adult to show you how.

Materials

Leather belt

Sticks

Oil

Penknife

Whetstone

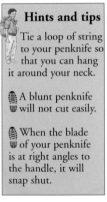

Hints and tips

Tie a loop of string to your penknife so that you can hang it around your neck.

🥾 A blunt penknife will not cut easily.

🥾 When the blade of your penknife is at right angles to the handle, it will snap shut.

The parts of a penknife

A saw and bottle opener are useful extras to have on a penknife.

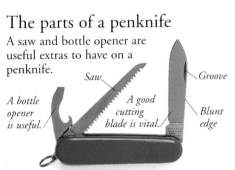

Saw

A bottle opener is useful.

A good cutting blade is vital.

Groove

Blunt edge

Making a sharp wooden point

You may want to make different kinds of gadgets for your camp. Once you know how to make a sharp point, you can adapt this technique to make all kinds of gadgets.

Strips of wood

Hold the wood firmly.

1 Always cut away from you so that if the penknife slips, you will not cut yourself. Cut several thin strips of wood rather than one large chunk.

Push the blade in at a 30 degree angle to make a sharp point.

2 Use the ball of your thumb to gently push the blade away from you. Continue cutting small strips of wood until you get a sharp point.

How to open and close a penknife safely

Put the nail of your thumb in the groove on the blunt edge of the blade.

Gently pull the blade as far as it will go. You should feel it click into place.

To close the penknife, put the fingers of one hand flat against the blunt side of the blade.

Gently push the blade the handle. Make sure fingers of your o are not in the way

How to sharpen the blade of a penknife safely

Rub some oil or water into the whetstone. Hold the sharp edge of the blade against the stone.

Stroke both sides of the sharp edge gently along the stone until the blade is very sharp.

Smooth the rough areas of this sharp edge by sweeping the blade up and down a leather belt.

Use the inside of the belt and always sweep the sharp edge of the knife away from you.

Stripping a branch

The branches you find lying on the ground will not always be exactly the shape you want. By stripping them, you can adapt them in any way you like.

1 Strip any leaves off the branch and snap off any brittle twigs. Now decide which twigs you want to keep. If you are making a pot hook (see page 26), you will need to keep the twigs at the bottom of the branch.

2 Use the penknife to remove any other twigs you do not want. Hold the blade with the sharp edge away from you. Cut the twig at its base, pushing the penknife away from the branch.

3 When you remove the twigs, you will be left with small stubs. Trim these down with your penknife. You can also strip the bark by gently sliding the blade of your penknife along the bark at a slight angle.

🥾 A branch with no bark will dry out much faster than one with bark.

How to use the small saw on a penknife

If you need to cut through a thick piece of wood, use the saw on the penknife.

Hold the saw upright because if it is at an angle, you will not have much control.

Pull and push the saw forward and backward until you have cut right through the branch.

Other cutting tools

If you are camping with an adult, you could ask him or her to make additional cutting tools.

🥾 Ask an adult to use these tools.

Making a wire saw
Bend a loop in each end of a [...] tach loops of [...] the ends of the wire.

Using a wire saw
Use the looped pieces of string as handles, and pull the wire backward and forward.

Cutting with flint
Sharpen flint by dropping it on a rock. The flint will break, giving a sharp cutting edge.

Useful knots I

There are hundreds of knots, each with different uses. However, certain knots have more than one use. It is better to learn just a few of these knots, rather than lots that you may forget or tie incorrectly. Also, make sure the string or rope you tie your knot with is strong enough for its purpose.

Reef knots are used when ropes might get wet and be hard to untie.

Materials

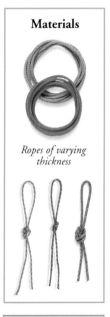

Ropes of varying thickness

Hints and tips

Tying a half-hitch knot on the end of another knot will make it stronger.

Tie a half-hitch knot into the end of a rope made from natural fibers to stop it from fraying.

Artificial-fiber ropes will not rot as easily as natural-fiber ropes.

Natural-fiber ropes are easier to handle when it is wet and icy.

Tying a figure-eight knot

This knot can be tied very quickly and is very strong. It is good for tying loops.

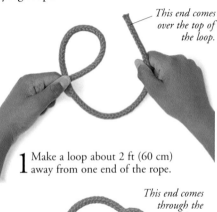

This end comes over the top of the loop.

1 Make a loop about 2 ft (60 cm) away from one end of the rope.

This end comes through the loop.

2 Take the long, loose end over the top of the rope and the loop, then through the loop to make a figure-eight shape.

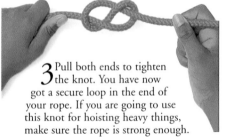

3 Pull both ends to tighten the knot. You have now got a secure loop in the end of your rope. If you are going to use this knot for hoisting heavy things, make sure the rope is strong enough.

How to tie a reef knot with two pieces of rope or string

Take two pieces of rope and bring the right piece of rope over and under the left piece.

Bring the red piece of rope on the left over the yellow piece on the right.

Tuck the red piece of rope under the yellow piece. Pull on both pieces of rope to secure the knot.

You can undo this knot easily by pushing the two ends of rope toward each other.

How to tie a half-hitch knot in a piece of rope or string

This knot is used to start many other knots and is handy for tying up loose ends. Make a loop.

Bring the right-hand side of the rope through the back of the loop and to the front of it.

Now pull both ends of the rope tight. This will secure and finish the half-hitch knot.

See page 16 if you need to seal the end of a rope made of artificial fibers.

Tying a bowline knot

A bowline knot will not slip or tighten, making it good for tying safety loops when climbing or diving.

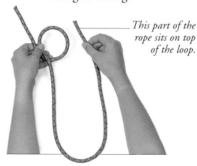

This part of the rope sits on top of the loop.

End of the rope

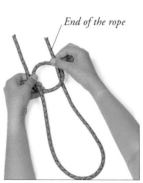

1 Decide how big the loop needs to be. You cannot change its size once you have tied the knot. Now make the loop.

2 Bring the end of the rope through the loop you have just made.

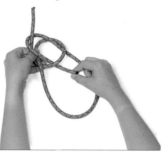

3 Bring the end of the rope around the top of the rope and then back through the loop.

4 Now pull on the top of the rope to tighten the knot. This will secure the loop.

Tying a sheet bend knot

Joining two ropes together requires a knot that will not slip, even if the ropes are different thicknesses. A sheet bend knot is the best one to use.

Make the loop in the thickest rope.

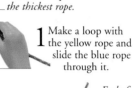

1 Make a loop with the yellow rope and slide the blue rope through it.

Keep the blue rope on top of the yellow rope.

End of blue rope

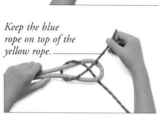

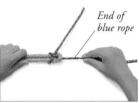

2 Bring the blue rope around the back of the looped yellow rope.

3 Tuck the end of the blue rope underneath the part of it that crosses the looped yellow rope.

4 Pull the end of the blue rope tight. The two ropes are now tied together securely.

Useful knots II

The knots you use to tie sticks together are called lashings. There are many different kinds of lashings, each of which is suitable for a certain job. For example, shear lashing is ideal for joining two sticks to make a long pole, and square lashing is ideal for joining sticks at right angles to each other.

A timber hitch knot is the best knot for starting a lashing with.

Materials

String

Rope

Penknife

Hints and tips

When tying diagonal lashing, wrap the string around both sticks three times in each diagonal.

🐚 Leaving one end of the string loose (instead of tucking it in) will enable you to undo the lashing more easily.

🐚 Make a walking stick by attaching a small stick to one end of a longer stick with square lashing.

🐚 You can use shear lashing to make a secure tripod. Lash three sticks together and pull the string down between each stick.

Tying a timber hitch knot

Both square and diagonal lashings start with a timber hitch knot. This knot is a variation of a standard half-hitch knot.

Short end of string

Long end of string

Loop

1 Use a piece of string to make a loop around a stick. Bring the long end of the string around the back of the short end.

Weave the long end of the string around the loop to make a twisted shape.

2 Twist the long end of the string in and out of the loop as many times as you can. You should be able to make three or four twists.

3 Now tighten the knot by gently pulling on the short end until the knot fits snugly around the stick. This knot can now form the basis of a lashing.

Short end of string

How to tie diagonal lashing on two sticks being pulled apart

Tie the string to one stick with a timber hitch knot. Wrap the string diagonally around both sticks.

Bring the string around the upright stick. Then wrap it around the sticks in the opposite diagonal.

Now bring the string around the front and b of the sticks in a circular shape three times.

Wrap the string ar the upright st secure it. hitch knot.

How to tie square lashing to two sticks crossing at right angles

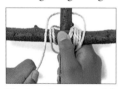

Tie the string to one stick with a timber hitch knot. Then start wrapping the string around both sticks.

Bring the string above and below both sticks in a circular movement three to four times.

Loop the string around one stick and wrap it around both sticks in the opposite direction.

When you have done this three to four times, secure the string with a clove hitch knot.

Tying shear lashing

Use this lashing to join two sticks that are parallel to each other.

1 Tie the string to one stick with a clove hitch knot. Then follow the detailed instructions, right.

Strong string will make the lashing even more secure.

2 Wrap the string around both sticks. You need to cover about 1 in (3 cm) of the sticks. Now bring the string downward between both sticks (see the detailed instructions, right.)

3 To make an A-frame shelter, pull the sticks apart at the bottom to make a triangular shape. You could make the shelter shown on page 16 stronger by using two sets of lashed sticks.

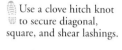

More details on how to tie shear lashing

Wrap the string around one stick several times. Then start wrapping it around both sticks.

Wrap the string tightly around both sticks. Make sure the string does not overlap.

Wrap the string in between both sticks three times. This will secure the lashing.

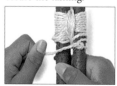

Secure the lashing by tying the string to one of the sticks with a clove hitch knot.

ing a clove hitch knot

this knot to tie string around i other solid objects.

Use a clove hitch knot to secure diagonal, square, and shear lashings.

 the string around . Keep one d.

2 Wrap the end facing upward around the stick, and tuck the end through the loop.

3 Finish the clove hitch knot by pulling both ends of the string tight.

First aid I

You can help a sick or injured person get better much faster if you know what to do immediately. This is called first aid. You need to be able to recognize when an injury is serious so you know to get help. If an injury is not serious, you need to know how to treat it so that it does not become infected.

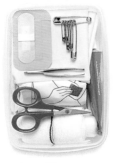

A first aid kit can prevent small injuries from becoming infected.

Contents of a first aid kit

If you are going hiking or are camping away from home, it is very important to take a first aid kit with you. The items shown here are all very useful things to have in your kit. Make sure you pack them in a clean, waterproof container.

Safety pins are useful for securing bandages.

Large bandages are useful for wrapping around injured arms and legs.

Gauze pads come in sealed paper wrappers, making them sterile, or germ-free.

Antiseptic wipes will disinfect broken skin.

Triangular bandages can be used as slings.

Conforming bandages shape themselves to fit into the curves of your body.

Adhesive bandages help keep cuts and scrapes clean.

Tweezers are useful for pulling out splinters and stings.

Corn pads will help protect any blisters on your feet.

Scissors are useful for cutting gauze and bandages.

Calamine lotion soothes sunburned skin.

How to treat cuts and scrapes with a gauze pad

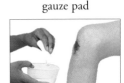

Gently wash the scrape with soap and water. Do this with a clean gauze pad.

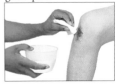

Try to remove any bits of dirt or gravel. Be very gentle – this may cause a little fresh bleeding.

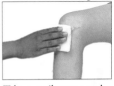

Take a sterile gauze pad and apply pressure to the cut or scrape to stop it from bleeding.

Put a bandage on the cut or scrape, making sure it has a pad large enough to cover the wound.

How to treat a wasp sting with tweezers and a cold compress

You will need a pair of tweezers to pull out the sting. Hold the injured area to keep it still.

Using the tweezers, grasp the sting as close to the skin as possible and pull it out.

Cool the area with a cold compress for about 10 minutes. Soaked gauze makes a good compress.

If the patient is stung in the mouth, give him or her cold water to drink and get an adult.

How to remove a splinter with tweezers

Wash around the splinter.   *Make sure the water is not too hot.*

1 Wash the affected area with soap and warm water. Be careful not to push the splinter in any farther.

2 With a pair of clean tweezers, grasp the splinter as close to the skin as possible and draw it out at the angle that it went in.

3 Squeeze the wound to encourage a little fresh bleeding. This will flush out any dirt. Wash the area again, pat it dry, and put a bandage on it.

How to treat burns and scalds and protect them from dirt

Run cold water over the injured area until it stops stinging. This will take at least 10 minutes.

Cover the burn with a clean plastic bag. If the skin is not broken, you can also use gauze.

Secure the bag loosely with a piece of tape. Ensure the bag and tape do not touch the burn.

Remember never to put any lotions or creams on the burn or scald.

Treating blisters

Foot blisters are very common when you are hiking. To prevent them, wear properly fitting socks and boots, and protect your feet with bandages as soon as they start to feel sore.

1 Clean the blister thoroughly with soap and water. Rinse it with clean warm water.

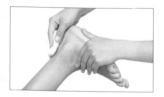

2 Dry the blister and the skin surrounding it by gently patting it with a clean pad.

3 Protect the blister with a bandage that has a pad large enough to cover the affected area.

4 If the blister is very large, cover it with a clean dressing. A gauze pad is ideal.

First aid II

You can save someone's life if you know what to do and act quickly. However, if you are unsure about anything, it is much safer to get adult help immediately. If someone is injured in a place that is dangerous for you to get to, you must get adult help immediately, even if you do know what to do.

If the patient has hypothermia, wrap him or her up warmly.

Have a cold drink.

Getting too hot or cold
When you are outdoors, your body is more sensitive to changes in temperature. You must be careful because getting too hot or cold can be very dangerous.

Treating sunburn
Sunburn occurs when you have been in the sun too long without protection. If you get sunburned, move into shade immediately and apply a soothing cream, such as calamine lotion.

Lie the affected person down in a cool place.

Sunburned skin is red and itchy, and feels tender.

Fanning will help cool him or her down.

⭐ If your skin starts to blister or bleed, see a doctor immediately.

Leave the water to dry naturally.

Treating heatstroke
Heatstroke can occur when the body gets very overheated. The affected person may get a headache and feel dizzy and hot. Bring the patient into the shade and remove any outer clothing. Sponge him or her with cool water until the body temperature returns to normal.

Treating hypothermia
Hypothermia can occur if the body temperature falls. It can be very dangerous. The affected person will shiver and feel cold. The most important thing is to heat him or her up. Wrap warm clothes and blankets around him or her, making sure the head is covered. Give the patient a warm drink and some high-energy food.

⭐ Do not apply direct heat, such as a hot water bottle, to the patient. He or she must warm up gradually.

If you do not have a blanket, wrap the patient in a sleeping bag.

How to recognize sunburn, heatstroke, and hypothermia

Sunburned skin looks red and sweaty. In extreme cases it may even start bleeding and blistering.

Heatstroke makes the skin flushed and dry. The heart beats fast, making the pulse rate increase.

Hypothermia slows down the heartbeat and pulse. The skin feels cold and looks pale and dry.

⭐ Ask someone to stay with the patient and get adult help immediately.

How to check someone's airway, breathing, and pulse

Check there is nothing in the mouth blocking the airway. Lift the jaw up and tilt the head back.

Check the breathing. Feel for breath on your cheek and watch to see if the chest rises up and down.

Gently press two fingers on the side of the windpipe to feel for a throb of pressure. This is the pulse.

⭐ If the patient's pulse and/or breathing does not seem normal, get adult help immediately.

Hints and tips

The windpipe, or airway, runs down the center of the neck to the lungs.

If the patient's breathing is very shallow, place a mirror under his or her mouth. The mirror will cloud over as he or she breathes.

Make notes about the patient's condition so that you can tell an adult exactly what has happened.

Finding someone unconscious

Shout to check the person is not just sleeping.

An unconscious person will be lying down, not moving. Use the instructions to the left to check for obstructions, breathing, and a pulse. Next, follow the instructions below to put the person into the recovery position. Then get adult help.

1 Lie the person on his or her back. Tilt the head back and lift the chin forward to ensure the airway is kept clear. Kneel in front and bend the arm nearest you to make a right angle.

Straighten the legs.

⭐ If you think the person may have a neck injury, get adult help immediately.

The palm must face upward.

The hand supports the face.

2 Bring the other arm across the chest. Hold the back of the hand against the cheek closest to you.

Hold the hand against the cheek.

Bend the leg at the knee.

3 With your free hand, hold the thigh farthest away from you. Gently pull the knee up to bend the leg, making sure you leave the foot flat on the ground.

Keep this leg straight.

Make sure the lower leg is still straight.

Use your knees to stop him or her from rolling over too far.

4 Continue holding the hand against the cheek. This will support the head. Pull the bent leg toward you so that the person rolls onto his or her side.

⭐ As soon as the patient is in the recovery position, get adult help.

5 Gently place the side of the face on the ground, keeping the hand underneath. Pull the top leg out to form a right angle. This will stop him or her from rolling over. Tilt the head back to make sure the airway is still open.

Outdoor Code

When you are outdoors, it is important to follow the Outdoor Code. This code tells you what you should and should not do to make sure that the countryside remains a place for everyone to enjoy. The most important points to remember are to respect wild animals and plants, and to take all of your garbage home with you.

What you should do

Make sure you wear light-colored clothes at night so that you can be seen easily. This is particularly important if you are walking on a roadside.

Reflectors and fluorescent bands will make you more visible at night.

Always close gates behind you. This ensures that animals cannot escape from their fields.

Always walk around fields if there is no path through. If you walk across them, you may damage crops.

Fields often look empty in the spring, but there may be crops sprouting.

You should always be wary of animals. Make sure you find out about any that may be dangerous in your area.

This rattlesnake is one of the fastest killers in the animal world.

A startled rattlesnake sounds a warning with a rattle on the tip of its tail.

Be very careful with any fire you light; fire can easily get out of control.

Even small fires, like this one, can spread very quickly.

The headlights on the front of a car will light up the road ahead.

If you are walking along a road, always make sure that you are facing the traffic on your side of the road. This is so that drivers can see you more easily, and so you can see them coming.

Make sure you keep your pet on a leash so that it does not run around and frighten other animals.

What you should avoid

Take all of your garbage home with you. Never throw it into rivers, ponds, or gutters, where animals might drink.

Never pick leaves or pull up plants; it is destructive and, in some places, illegal.

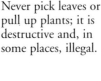

This mother will be very protective of her young lambs.

Do not force your way through fences, walls, or hedges; if you damage them, animals could escape.

You must not chase animals; they may hurt themselves or even turn on you.

Try not to make too much noise and don't play a radio or tape player. Loud noises will disturb other people and animals.

Useful addresses

Girl Scouts of the USA
420 Fifth Avenue
New York, NY 10018-2798
(800) 247-8319

Boy Scouts of America
PO Box 152079
Irving, TX 75015-2079
(214) 580-2000

Boys & Girls Clubs of America
1230 West Peachtree Street, NW
Atlanta, Georgia 30309-3494
(800) 854-CLUB (2582)

Camp Fire Boys and Girls
4601 Madison Avenue
Kansas City, MO 64112-1278
(816) 756-1950

YMCA
101 North Wacker Drive
Chicago, Illinois 60606
(312) 977-0031
(800) 872-9622

YWCA
726 Broadway
New York, NY 10003
(212) 614-2700

Scouts Canada
National Headquarters
P.O. Box 5151, Stn. F
Ottawa, Ontario
K2C 3G7
(613) 224-5131

Girl Guides of Canada
50 Merton Street
Toronto, Ontario
M4S 1A3
(416) 487-5281

4-H Club
Contact your local County Extension
Service (under Government section in phone
book) and ask for your local 4-H chapter.

L.L. Bean
L.L. Bean, Incorporated
Freeport, ME 04033
(800) 341-4341 (customer service)
(800) 221-4221 (order dept.)

Patagonia
1609 West Babcock
Bozman, MT 59715
(800) 638-6464

R.E.I. (Recreational Equipment Incorporated)
1700 45th Street
Sumner, WA 98390
(800) 327-8852

Index

A

altocumulus
 cloud 51
altostratus
 cloud 50
animals, tracks 48

B

backpack 12, 13
bag, how to
 make 13
bark rubbing 47
bearings 36
Big Dipper, the 42
blisters, how to
 treat 59
bowline knot 55
breathing, how
 to check 61
burns, how to
 treat 59

C

camp pillow 22
camp shower 21
camp stool 33
cirrocumulus
 cloud 50
cirrostratus
 cloud 50
cirrus cloud 50
clean-up gear 11
clothesline 19
clothespin 19
clove hitch
 knot 57

contour map 38
cumulonimbus
 cloud 51
cumulus cloud 51
cuts and grazes,
 how to treat 58

D, E

damper bread 30
diagonal lashing 56
domed tent 15

F

figure-eight
 knot 54
first aid kit 58
flag signals,
 sending 45

G

gaiters 8

garbage,
 storing 21
grill 31

H

half-hitch knot 55
hanging pantry 20
heatstroke, how
 to treat 60
hill-stratus
 cloud 51
hoof print 48

hopping print 48
hypothermia,
 how to treat 60

I, J, K

kindling 25

L, M, N

layer principle 8
legend 38
lichen 46
map case 41
mud scraper 33
nocturnal animals
 49

O, P, Q

paw print 48
penknife, how
 to sharpen 53
pot hook 26
protractor
 compass 37
pulse, how to
 check 61

R

rain gauge 51
recovery
 position 61
reef knot 54
resuscitation 61
ridge tent 15
route card, how
 to make 40

S

shear lashing 57
sheet bag 23
sheet bend knot 55
sleeping bag 23
sleeping mat 22
Southern Cross,
 the 42
splinter, how to
 remove 59
square lashing 57
sterilizing
 tablets 34
stratocumulus
 cloud 51
sun dial 43
sunburn, how
 to treat 60
survival kit 10

T, U, V

tepee fire 24
timber hitch
 knot 56
tinder 25
tripod, how to
 make 26
tunnel tent 15

W, X, Y, Z

wading print 48
washing gear 11
wasp sting, how
 to remove 59
water collector 35
wind gauge
 50
wire saw
 53

Acknowledgments
DK would like to thank :

Erik Warren and Nick Dewdney for advice
at photographic sessions; Gary Sanders for
reviewing the synopsis; Carole Stott for
checking the *Using the Sun and stars* pages;
Brian Cosgrove for checking the *Weather watch*
pages; Dr. Rachel Carroll and Dr. Simon Carroll
for advice on first aid procedures; and Y.H.A.
Adventure Shops for lending equipment.

Picture research: Jo Walton
Picture credits: T top; B bottom; C center;
L left; R right;
Brian Cosgrove: 50 TR, CR, CRB & BR, 51TL,
CLT, CL, CLB & BL,
John Cleare/Mountain Camera: 15TR & CR
Cartography: Roger Bullen, James Anderson
Illustrations: Nick Hewetson, John Woodcock